EASY INSTRUMENTAL DUETS VIOLINS

CHRISTMAS CAROLS FOR TWO

T0039455

Arrangements by Mark Phillips

ISBN 978-1-5400-2920-1

HAL•LEONARD®

Contact Us:
Hal Leonard
7777 West Bluemound Road
Milwaukee, WI 53213
Email: info@halleonard.com

In Europe contact:
Hal Leonard Europe Limited
Distribution Centre, Newmarket Road
Bury St Edmunds, Suffolk, IP33 3YB
Email: info@halleonardeurope.com

In Australia contact:
Hal Leonard Australia Pty. Ltd.
4 Lentara Court
Cheltenham, Victoria, 3192 Australia
Email: info@halleonard.com.au

CONTENTS

ANGELS WE HAVE HEARD ON HIGH

VIOLINS

Traditional French Carol

21
25
29
33
36
39

AWAY IN A MANGER

VIOLINS

Music by James R. Murray

17
21
25
29

BRING A TORCH, JEANNETTE, ISABELLA

VIOLINS

17th Century French Provençal Carol

12
16
20
24

DECK THE HALL

VIOLINS

Traditional Welsh Carol

17
21
24
27
30

THE FIRST NOEL

VIOLINS

17th Century English Carol
Music from W. Sandys' *Christmas Carols*

17
21
25
29

GO, TELL IT ON THE MOUNTAIN

VIOLINS

African-American Spiritual

21
25
29
33
37

GOD REST YE MERRY, GENTLEMEN

VIOLINS

Traditional English Carol

20
24
28
31
35

HARK! THE HERALD ANGELS SING

VIOLINS

Music by Felix Mendelssohn-Bartholdy
Arranged by William H. Cummings

21
25
29
33
37

IT CAME UPON THE MIDNIGHT CLEAR

VIOLINS

Music by Richard Storrs Willis

17
21
25
29

JINGLE BELLS

VIOLINS

Words and Music by J. Pierpont

Brightly, in 2

17
21
25
29

JOLLY OLD ST. NICHOLAS

VIOLINS

Traditional 19th Century American Carol

17
21
25
29

JOY TO THE WORLD

VIOLINS

Music by George Frideric Handel
Adapted by Lowell Mason

20
24
28
32
35

O CHRISTMAS TREE

VIOLINS

Traditional German Carol

17
21
25
29

O COME, ALL YE FAITHFUL

VIOLINS

Music by John Francis Wade

Moderately

21
25
29
33
37

O COME, O COME, EMMANUEL

VIOLINS

15th Century French Melody
Adapted by Thomas Helmore

Moderately slow, in 2

20
24
27
31
35

O HOLY NIGHT

VIOLINS

Music by Adolphe Adam

26
31
36
41
46

O LITTLE TOWN OF BETHLEHEM

VIOLINS

Music by Lewis H. Redner

17
20
23
26
29

SILENT NIGHT

VIOLINS

Music by Franz X. Gruber

25
29
34
39
44

STILL, STILL, STILL

VIOLINS

Salzburg Melody, c.1819

13
16
19
22
25

WE THREE KINGS OF ORIENT ARE

VIOLINS

Words and Music by John H. Hopkins, Jr.

17
21
25
29

WE WISH YOU A MERRY CHRISTMAS

VIOLINS

Traditional English Folksong

21
25
29
33
37

WHAT CHILD IS THIS?

VIOLINS

16th Century English Melody

31
37
42
47
53
59